TABLE OF CONTENTS

OUT OF THE DARKNESS

There are many horrors to be found in the realm of darkness; werewolves, those evil man-beasts who attack unsuspecting travelers with their bare teeth; zombies, climbing out of fresh graves — undead souls marching to death's drummer. The princes of darkness themselves, vampires, whose very life depends on the drinking of human blood.

Since the dawn of time, these creatures of the night have merged from the shadows, casting a pall of dread on the innocent. Are the perplexing stories of vampires, werewolves, and zombies folktales with no basis in fact? Or are these bizarre oddities as real as you and me?

In recent years, scientists have discovered that vampires, zombies, and wolf-people could exist. Stories of them have appeared in history. Some say these beasts walk the earth today. Some of these poor souls have rare diseases, some have had chemical curses put on them by voodoo priests, and some are just plain weird. So many legends have been told about these night creatures from Transylvania to Haiti to

Hollywood, that it is hard to separate fact from fiction. But it is time to set the story straight. So dim the lights, pull the shades, and ready yourself for some blood-curdling facts about vampires, werewolves, and zombies.

VAMPIRES —
BLOODY FIENDS OF HISTORY

There is no way of knowing when the first vampire stalked the night in search of a drink of human blood. One of the earliest fables of a vampire-like creature is the story of Lilith, from ancient Babylonia. According to legend, Lilith was the first wife of Adam, in the Garden of Eden. When Lilith refused to obey Adam, she was banished from Eden as punishment. Thereafter, she became a demon of the night and a haunter of darkness. The saga of Lilith says that she struck terror in the hearts of people by swooping down out of the sky to suck the blood of helpless children.

Another blood-drinking monster from antiquity is Lamia, from ancient Greece. Lamia had the head of a woman and the scaly body of a winged serpent. Like Lilith, she dropped out of the sky. Lamia was adopted by the Romans and called the Strix. The plural of the word Strix is "stregae" a word that found its way into the Italian language and means "witch."

From ancient Greece, Lamia was a winged serpent with the head of a woman.

Vampire myths are part of almost every culture on Earth. They can be found in China, where monsters with blazing red eyes, razor-sharp talons, and green hair, drink their victims's blood and then devour their bodies. Fables from Japan tell of a monstrous vampire-cat, who kills its victim, buries the body, and transforms itself into the dead person. This evil cat then goes to the home of its victim and snacks on the relatives.

In Malaysia there is an exotic vampire called a Langsuir, who appears as a beautiful woman in a flowing green robe. Her nails are long and sharp and she has jet black hair down to her ankles. She drinks the blood of children through a hole in the back of her neck. The Langsuir can be rendered harmless if someone cuts her nails and hair. The hair must then be stuffed into the hole in her neck.

Some Malaysians believed that women were in danger of becoming Languirs after death. To prevent this, after Malaysian women died, they were buried with glass beads in their mouths, eggs in their armpits, and needles in their palms. Then, they could not open their mouths to scream or flap their arms to fly. Malaysian myths include at least three more vampire-like creatures, as does Indian mythology.

Vampire myths are part of almost every culture on Earth.

The most loathsome vampires in the world are the European variety, for they are evil incarnate. The ghastly descriptions of vampires from European folklore tax the imagination and may send the listener running for a breath of fresh air.

The face of the vampire is pale but lifelike and its eyes are glazed, glinting, and glaring. The vampire's mouth is a hideous gaping maw, full of gleaming, razor-sharp teeth. Black, clotted blood stains the chin and the corners of the mouth. The breath of a vampire emits an indescribably wretched stench.

THE REAL-LIFE VAMPIRE

Almost everyone has heard of Dracula, the bloodsucking Transylvanian vampire of book and movie fame. Most people do not know that the story of Dracula, written by Bram Stoker, is loosely based on a real person who ruled Transylvania, Romania, over five hundred years ago.

Vlad Dracula became the prince of Transylvania in 1456. At that time, Transylvania was involved in a series of vicious regional wars. Life was cheap and death was always at hand during those bitter years. Vlad Dracula was a blood-thirsty tyrant, a fiendish man who found his joy in the agony of others.

To understand Vlad Dracula better, one only need look at the origins of his name . In the local language of Romania, "Dracula" has the double meaning of "devil" and "dragon." Another name Vlad acquired was "Tepes," which means "the impaler." "Impale" means to torture or kill with a sharpened stake thrust up through the body. How did Vlad ever get such an ominous nickname? The answer is chillingly simple. Vlad Dracula's favorite means of punishment for those who displeased him was to impale them alive on a stake.

Impale Vlad did. First, were the victims of his wars. Near the citadel of Giurgiu on the Danube River, Vlad impaled over twenty thousand war prisoners from Bulgaria, Hungary, Germany, and Turkey. When the Turkish army walked through the forest of impaled corpses, they were sickened and demoralized by the grisly sight.

When Vlad assumed the throne in 1456, he had over five hundred members of his court impaled as a lesson to those who would doubt him. One of Vlad's most notorious depravities occurred on April 2, 1459. On that lovely spring day, Dracula had thousands of Saxon townsfolk impaled in a huge circle around him and his court. In the middle sat Vlad, feasting on venison and wine.

On another occasion, two Turkish diplomats refused to remove their turbans in Vlad's presence. Dracula ordered his henchman to nail the turbans onto the diplomat's heads so they could never be removed again.

The death of Vlad Dracula the Impaler is steeped in mystery. Some say he was killed in a battle with the Turks. Others say he was killed by his own men. Whatever the story, Dracula ended his bloody career in 1476. His head was chopped off and sent to the Turkish capital of Constantinople where it was placed on public display to advertise that the evil butcher, was now dead.

THE CRAZED COUNTESS

In the late 1500s, Elisabeth Bathory, a beautiful and insane Hungarian countess, thought she had discovered the secret to eternal beauty — bathing in the blood of young peasant girls. Year after year, the Countess Bathory thrived on her daily bloodbaths, convinced that they were the reason for her good looks.

When the countess tired of peasant girls, she decided she needed young noblewomen for her cursed baths. In 1610, twenty-five noblewomen were brought to the countess' castle. Within two weeks they were dead as a result of the daily bloodbaths. This gave the royalty the excuse they needed to put the countess on trial. At the time, killing peasant girls was not against the law. But killing noblewomen could not be allowed. Bathory was tried and convicted of murder. At the trial, it was revealed that the Countess Bathory had personally murdered six-hundred-and-fifty girls, many of whom she had bitten to death in the neck.

Although the king wanted to behead the countess at once, her high position in the royal family would not allow it. A compromise was reached. The fifty-year-old Elisabeth, her fabled beauty now faded, was walled up alive in a tower room in her castle. Slits were left for air and the passage of food and water. After four years in the wall, the countess died. The townspeople were still not convinced that the butcher Bathory was dead. They thought her soul might have turned to smoke and escaped her walled prison. Old myths die hard. Today, her bones lay untouched in the castle ruins in the Czechoslovakian town of Chactice.

The Countess of Bathory was walled up alive in a tower room in her castle.

VAMPIRES TODAY

Dracula and the Countess Bathory are just two of the thousands of diabolical vampires who have lived. The twisted tales of every vampire atrocity would fill hundreds of books, and if you think that tales of vampires come from dusty old history texts, think again. A survey taken in 1983, called the Last Official Vampire Estimate, or LOVE Survey, says that there are an estimated two hundred "physical vampires" in the United States and over five hundred worldwide. According to the LOVE survey, reprinted in *American Demographics* magazine, there is even a vampire on the White House staff in Washington!

Vampires, like everyone else, seem to have adapted to the 20th century. Killing is definitely a no-no. Now, most of them exist on blood donated by friends. One Florida vampire, who owns apartment buildings, exchanges free rent for blood donations. In 1983, the top state for vampires was California with ten.

Modern vampires still have an image problem, being connected with people like the Countess

Bathory. But like Bathory, some vampires claim that drinking blood keeps them from aging. One man claims to be seven hundred years old. He also claims that he cannot be photographed or seen in mirrors because he is "soulless." Modern vampires also have adapted to going out in the sunlight. While a few still shun daylight, many are able to soak it up. They say it recharges their batteries.

Vampires claim to be soulless and they shun away from sunlight.

WEREWOLVES

A howl in the night pierces the silence. By the light of the full moon a man shambles across a field. As the moments pass, the man begins to grow fangs, his eyes glaze red, and hair begins to grow all over his face. The man is turning into a crazed animal. His clothes rip away as his body sinew turns into that of a wolf's. His human brain is gone and he hears only one thing in his mind, "Blood! Blood! Blood!"

Small animals skitter out of the werewolf's reach. A few unfortunate animals are caught by the beast and he shreds them apart, feasting on the raw meat. Blood drips from his fangs. Ominously, the beast pauses and sniffs the air.

A young woman is approaching, returning home after visiting her mother. The beast creeps behind a tree. From his mouth comes a steady series of gasping snorts and snarls. Flies swarm around the carnage on his chin. The woman draws nearer.

Werewolf myths are so common that the study of werewolfism has a name, lycanthropy.

From behind the tree, the werewolf leaps, grabbing the screaming woman with his razor claws, throwing her to the ground and setting to work on her flesh. Within moments, the beast's thirst is quenched as the woman's lifeblood runs from her body.

The night has teeth, the night has claws, and the night has a thirst for blood. The dread of the werewolf has haunted the night since time began. Who wouldn't pale at the very thought of this man-beast? For what creature could be more frightening than one who walks the earth as a normal man by day and a savage brute by night?

Werewolf myths are so common that the study of werewolfism has a name, lycanthropy. "Lykos" is Greek for wolf, and "anthropos" for man. In Western cultures, the most common belief is that people may turn into wolves. In other cultures legends state that people turn into jaguars, foxes, tigers, hyenas, crocodiles, and even elephants. One of the more popular werewolf fables is that of "Little Red Riding Hood," where the big, bad wolf tries to eat Little Red Riding Hood.

While no one can prove that werewolves exist, people in Europe certainly believed they did.

France, Germany, and other countries passed laws making it illegal to turn into a werewolf. During the 16th and 17th centuries, men were brought before a jury because they broke this law.

One of the more celebrated wolfman trials occurred in Bordeaux, France in the 1700s. The werewolf's name was Jean Grenier. Some claimed he had killed and eaten over fifty young girls. It is interesting to note that when witches were tried during this period they were usually burned at the stake. Grenier was deemed insane and spent the rest of his days in a mental institution.

Some people believed that a person could become a werewolf by eating certain plants or drinking contaminated water. An old Irish legend says that St. Patrick sometimes punished people by turning them into wolves. A Welsh king suffered this curse, and he and his family turned into werewolves every seven years.

Perhaps the strangest tales of wolf-people are the stories about children who were lost in the woods and were raised by wolves. The ancient myth about Romulus and Remus tells of two boys who were raised by wolves. They later founded the city of Rome.

Scientists have documented cases of children who walked on all fours, ate like animals and could not speak. In Lithuania, in 1661, two little boys were found by a group of hunters. They had been raised in the woods by wolves. The hunters captured one boy, about nine years old, and took him to Warsaw, where he became the pet of the royal family. No one could teach the boy to speak or give up his wolfish nature. Several times he tried to escape into the woods and was once seen exchanging hugs with a wild bear.

There have also been tales of human children raised by bears, leopards, antelopes, goats, pigs, and sheep. In each case, the children acquired the habits, abilities, and even the features of their animal guardians. For reasons not understood, most of the time these children die before becoming teen-agers.

Scientist have documented cases of children who walked on all fours, ate like animals and could not speak.

ZOMBIES - BURIED ALIVE!

A man lies in his coffin. His funeral is happening around him. He can hear his sister crying as his friends file past his casket paying their last respects. The man is alive, but he cannot move. He sees, he feels, but he remains paralyzed. Soon, the funeral is over and a horse-drawn cart carries the man in his coffin to the graveyard. His mouth curls into a silent scream as the coffin lid is nailed shut and the casket is lowered. He feels the thud of the dirt being shoveled from above, burying him alive. Within minutes, all is darkness.

Twelve hours later the man can move again. He starts to scream in the absolute black coffin. Desperately, he claws at the walls of his casket, hopelessly trying to push back the six feet of dirt that entombs him. But wait. He hears digging! He is being rescued! Moments later, the man is violently jerked from his coffin, his wrists are tied together by two men who refill the grave. Then he is forced to eat a foul-tasting plant and loaded in a truck bound for a sugar cane farm. There, he will be a zombie farm slave with one hundred other unfortunate souls.

Is this a scene from a horror movie? Yes, but it is also reality for a man named Clairvius Narcisse, a former zombie on the tropical island of Haiti. Narcisse says that he was kept as a zombie slave for over two years. One day, his overseer forgot to give him and the other slaves the zombie drug. When they came out of their trance, the zombies killed the overseer and escaped.

Released from the effects of the zombie drug, Narcisse soon became his normal self. He didn't return home because he thought that his brother had arranged to make him a zombie. But after eighteen years, his brother died, and Clairvius Narcisse walked back into the lives of his friends and family who thought that he had been dead for nearly two decades. Narcisse may be one of the few people who have visited their own graves and seen their own name on a tombstone.

VOODOO AND MAGIC

The island of Haiti lies in the Caribbean Sea between Cuba and Puerto Rico. Columbus named Haiti's island Hispaniola when he first sailed there in 1492. The island eventually came under French possession in the 1700s. The French needed slaves to work their plantations in Haiti, and between 1780 and 1790, they imported over four hundred thousand slaves from Africa. Although the slaves were from all over Africa, they all carried with them a series of ancient religious beliefs, rituals, and magic. Over the years, these beliefs mingled together under the tropical sun and became known as voodoo, which means "study of the unknown."

The practice of voodoo was fiercely forbidden by the white slave owners and they used every cruel means available to restrict its practice. Imprisonment, lashings, hangings, and torture were common punishments for the slaves caught practicing their native religion. The struggle against voodoo continued for hundreds of years. Voodoo became more mysterious and secret. When Haiti won its independence in 1804, voodoo came out into the open. It is still practiced in the Caribbean and the southern United States, especially in Florida and Louisiana.

Voodoo ceremonies with singing, dancing, and drumming are held to summon and win the favor of one of the hundreds of voodoo gods or "Loa." At these ceremonies, people go into frenzied trances where they become possessed by the Loa. In this state, they might walk on burning coals, stick pins through their cheeks, or eat broken glass, all without bleeding or feeling pain. When the ceremony is over, the possessed people return to normal, often forgetting what happened. Miraculously, their bodies remain unscarred even after fire-walking and glass eating.

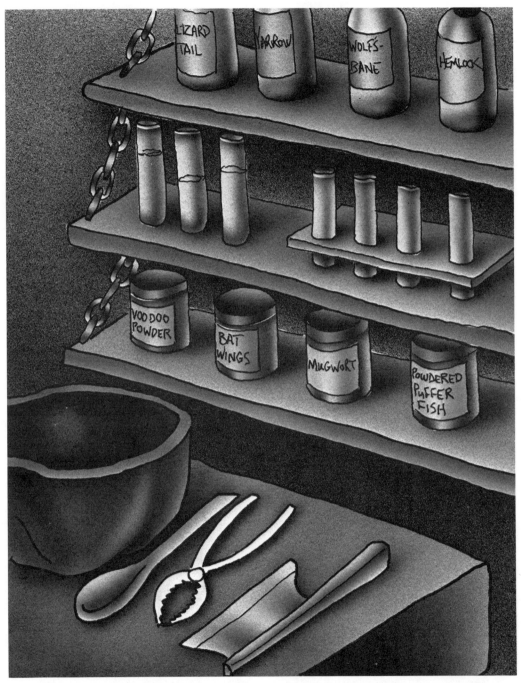

Voodoo priests use plants and herbs to cast spells.

HERBS, MAGIC, AND SPELLS

When Africans came to the New World in the 17th and 18th centuries, many of them had a knowledge of plants, herbs, and animals that voodoo priests use to cast spells. Most of these spells are rituals to attract money or love. Some herbal potions are used in voodoo ceremonies. But when a voodoo priest wants to use magic for evil, watch out!

What happened to Clairvius Narcisse has happened to thousands of other people who had enemies that, for one reason or another, wanted them "neutralized." In Narcisse's case, his brother wanted Narcisse's land holdings. Narcisse's brother went to a voodoo priest, called a "hougan," and had some zombie powder made. The hougan went to the cemetery, dug up a dead body, and collected some bone shavings from the corpse. The hougan then performed a magic ritual while mixing the bone shavings with other secret herbs. The hougan added the main ingredient, the burnt, powered remains of a puffer fish. Soon, the zombie powder was prepared. When the powder was blown in Narcisse's face, he was on his way to a living grave.

THE FISH OF DEATH

In recent years, scientists have studied zombie poisons hoping to learn their secrets. What they have discovered is that the puffer fish contains a poison that induces a sleep-like state when it is rubbed on the skin. The victim's breathing, along with heartbeat and pulse, slows. Within half an hour, the victim of puffer poisoning seems dead to all, including doctors. But if the dose is low enough, within twelve hours, the poison can wear off. By then it's too late, for the victims are already in their graves.

The zombies that are rescued from their graves in Haiti are given a plant called datura that keeps them as zombie-like slaves. If the datura is not given to the zombie, they return to normal, as in the case of Narcisse. Some people never recover, because the trauma of being buried alive makes them go insane.

Voodoo, with its magic and secret potions, is an important religion to almost everybody in Haiti. Out of the millions of people who practice voodoo, only a few people misuse its powers. The strange mysterious religion remains a driving force today.

Zombies are people who are poisoned and live in a sleep-like state.

WATCH OUT!

As you can see, history is full of tales of vampires, werewolves, and zombies. It seems that in past centuries, these bloody beasts were more common than they are today. In modern times, we know that a man can't turn into a wolf. Or do we? We believe that vampires don't really exist. But do we know for certain? For now, these questions still beg for an answer. So when you hear that howl in the night, BEWARE! It could just be the neighbor's dog. But are you really sure?